CONTENTS

Words that appear in the text in bold, **like this**, are explained in the Glossary.

N
W   E
S

AMAZON
RAINFOREST

Amazon River

Quito

TAMBO-
MACHAY

Cajamarca
Chan Chan

MACHU PICCHU

Pachacamac

Cuzco

LAKE TITICACA

A
N
D
E
S

M
O
U
N
T
A
I
N
S

SACSAHUAMAN

Tiahuanaco

PACIFIC OCEAN

North
America

Atlantic
Ocean

Central
America

Pacific
Ocean

South
America

INCA EMPIRE

ATLANTIC OCEAN

MAP OF THE INCA EMPIRE

The ruins of the Inca city of Machu Picchu, high in the Andes mountains.

CHAPTER 1

FACTS ABOUT THE INCA EMPIRE

Do you have a head for heights, strong legs, and a sense of adventure? Do you enjoy spectacular scenery and colourful ceremonies, and not mind walking for days on end? If the answer to all these questions is yes, then a trip to the Inca Empire is the holiday for you.

The Inca Empire stretches right along the western coast of South America. It covers dramatic country, from stony deserts to high mountain peaks and steamy rainforests. You will find that the Inca Empire is very well run, with excellent roads. Altogether, a trip to the Inca lands will make you feel on top of the world!

WHEN TO TRAVEL

If you want to visit the Inca Empire, you only have 100 years in which to make your trip. Around 1430 the Incas settled in their city of Cuzco. Between 1438 and 1463, the Inca ruler Pachacuti built up a powerful **city-state** with Cuzco at its heart. Over the next 10 years, Pachacuti and his son Topa Inca conquered the Chimu people in the north. And by 1493, Topa Inca had trebled the size of his empire, winning vast stretches of land to the south.

This is an 18th century painting of the Emperor Atahualpa. His reign ended in tragedy for the Incas.

Between 1438 and 1493, the Inca army fought many fierce battles – so if you visit then, you'll need to stay away from areas of conflict. However, you'll find most people are busy working as farmers, fishermen, traders, and craft workers.

PEAK TIME

To catch the Inca Empire at its height, visit between 1493 and 1525. At this time Huayna Capac ruled the empire, and under him it reached its greatest size. If you visit at this time, you'll find a well run empire, with thriving cities and towns linked by a network of roads.

WHO WERE THE INCAS?

The name "Inca" actually only refers to the people who live in Cuzco. All the other people in the empire belong to different tribes or nations. They are often known as the Andean people because they live in the Andes region.

KEEP AWAY!

After 1525 the Inca Empire should be avoided. By then, the empire was divided by a bloody **civil war** as the sons of Huayna Capac fought each other for power. Then, in 1532, an expedition of Spanish **conquistadors**, led by Francisco Pizarro, arrived in Peru. Pizarro captured the Inca Emperor Atahualpa and later put him to death.

In 1572 the last Inca ruler was executed and Spain seized all the Inca lands. During this period you'll see the Spaniards treating the Incas cruelly. You'll also be at risk from **smallpox**, measles, and influenza, all brought from Europe by Spanish soldiers.

OTHER TIMES TO AVOID

Before you set off for the Inca Empire, check for **droughts**, earthquakes, volcanic eruptions, and the rainy season (from March to December). However, if you happen to arrive at a bad time, the Incas will be well prepared. All over the empire there are storehouses, filled with food and clothing in case of emergency.

GOOD AND BAD TIMES

1200–1300	The Incas settle in the Cuzco valley
1300–1400	The city of Cuzco grows
1438–63	Pachacuti Inca wins land around Cuzco
1463–71	Pachacuti and Topa Inca conquer the Chimu lands in the north
1471–93	Topa Inca conquers the southern part of the empire
1493–1525	Huayna Capac rules the empire and conquers more lands
1525–32	Civil war between the sons of Huayna Capac
1532–72	Francisco Pizarro and his Spanish army gradually take over the Inca Empire; smallpox, measles, and influenza kill millions; the Incas also suffer from **famine**

Key:

Stay away

Visit with caution

Best time to visit

Most of the coast of the Inca Empire is rocky, barren, and empty, but there are a few towns with great sea views.

GEOGRAPHY AND CLIMATE

The Inca Empire stretches in a long, narrow strip along the Pacific coast of South America. It measures around 4,800 km (3,000 miles) from north to south, and extends about 320 kilometres (200 miles) inland. If you want to see all of the empire, you'll need to cover hundreds of miles. Fortunately, the Incas have excellent roads!

A LAND OF CONTRASTS

You will be amazed by the range of stunning landscapes in the Inca Empire. Close to the coast are low-lying deserts. Further inland, the land rises steeply towards the snowy peaks of the Andes mountains. Beyond the mountains are dense **tropical** rainforests, with a maze of rivers draining into the mighty Amazon River.

During your trip you'll probably spend most of your time in the **fertile** valleys between the mountain peaks. This is where most of the major cities and towns are found, such as Cuzco and Machu Picchu. But don't forget to visit some coastal towns, too. Pachacamac, on the central coast, has some spectacular temples overlooking the sea.

WATCH THE WEATHER

You will need to come prepared for all kinds of weather in the Inca Empire. In the deserts it is burning hot during the day and icy cold at night. Meanwhile, in the rainforests it is always hot and steamy.

Up in the mountains, the weather is warm in the daytime but quickly turns colder late in the afternoon. At night it is freezing cold for most of the year, with sharp frosts, snow, and hail storms. The rainy season lasts from December to March, but there can also be long periods of drought, when all the crops wilt in the fields.

CRYING LLAMAS

In times of drought, farmers tie up their llamas without any drink. They believe that the desperate cries of the llamas will make the gods take pity on them and send them water.

DIFFERENT LIFESTYLES

Wherever you travel in the Inca Empire, you'll find people adapting to their different landscapes. On the steep mountainsides, farmers build narrow **terraced** fields, which they plant with potatoes and other **root vegetables** that can resist the cold. You'll also see herds of llamas in the high mountain **pastures**.

In the mountains, Inca farmers make the most of every inch of land, by cutting terraces into the hillside.

In the fertile valleys between the mountains, the fields are larger and the main crops are maize and beans. Here, many people live in towns or cities and work as craft workers. In the tropical regions further inland, farmers grow squashes, tomatoes, and fruit. On the sandy coasts, people survive by farming, fishing, and hunting birds.

WHO'S WHO IN THE INCA EMPIRE?

Before you head off to South America, it is a good idea to work out exactly who does what in the Inca Empire. Inca society is divided into strict social classes, so you'll need to know exactly how to treat the different kinds of people you meet.

SAPAS

At the very top of Inca society is the emperor, known as the Sapa Inca. The Incas believe that he is the son of the sun, and they treat him like a god. The Sapa Inca doesn't feed or dress himself, and instead of walking he is usually carried around in a **litter** (a throne held up by several servants). People entering the emperor's presence have to take off their shoes and carry a load on their back, to show that they are humble before him.

Everyone in the empire is expected to respect the Sapa Inca and worship him like a god. To make sure all his people stay loyal to him, the emperor makes many journeys throughout his lands. He is carried in a litter along the Inca roads, accompanied by a grand procession (see page 31). Everywhere the Sapa Inca goes, crowds of people gather to worship him.

The Sapa Inca wears colourful **embroidered** robes and a special headdress with a red fringe and golden tassels. But whatever you do, don't be tempted to stare at him. Anyone who dares to look the emperor in the face is instantly put to death!

GIRLS BEWARE!

Girls need to keep well away from the Sapa Inca. Wherever the Sapa Inca travels, he keeps a look out for girls to marry. If you are chosen to be one of his wives, you must obey or be put to death.

COYAS

The Sapa Inca has hundreds of wives, but his most important wife is his sister. She is called the Coya Inca and she is believed to be the daughter of the moon. By marrying his sister, the Sapa Inca believes that his children will have the pure blood of the sun. This is important because one of his sons will be the next emperor.

NOBLES AND COMMONERS

All the emperor's children automatically become nobles. Some nobles work as priests, judges, or army officers. Others are officials in the different regions of the empire.

This 18th century painting shows the first ever Coya, Mama Occlo.

It's easy to spot nobles by their dress. They have large gold earplugs (see page 18) and tunics made from very fine woven cloth. For special occasions, such as festivals, nobles wear tall, feathered headdresses. They also have golden medallions on their chests and heels, and cloaks made from glittering plates of silver and gold.

The ordinary people work as farmers, labourers, and craft workers. They have to work very hard and obey all the orders of the nobles. These hard-working people have a strong sense of community. They live in large family groups called *ayllus*, and all the members of an *ayllu* share the family's tasks. The *ayllu* is led by a group of elders, who decide on the rules for their community.

HOW THE INCA EMPIRE IS RUN

The Inca Empire is very well run. Some people even think it compares with the Roman Empire. The Empire is divided into four quarters, and each quarter has its own governor. These four governors hold regular meetings with the Sapa Inca and carry out his orders. Under the governors are hundreds of local officials. Their job is to make sure that everyone obeys the emperor's orders and that people do their duty of service to the empire.

SERVING THE EMPIRE

All the men in the Inca lands have to spend part of every year working for the empire. Many Incas serve the empire by working in the Fields of the Sun – the lands which belong to the emperor and priests. Some serve in the army (see page 53) or build roads, temples, and **fortresses**. Others help to transport goods around the empire or work in the **mines**, digging for gold, silver, or copper. Meanwhile, the Inca women support their men by cooking and weaving clothes. They also look after the children, as well as working on the land.

A CARING SOCIETY

In return for their services, the Inca Empire takes care of everyone in the Inca lands. If somebody becomes ill or is too old to work, the person is given shelter, clothes, and food. The Incas also plan ahead for disasters, such as floods, or famine. Large stone storehouses are kept stocked up with food, water, and clothing. These supplies are distributed in times of emergency. The Incas are very proud of the fact that nobody is forced to go hungry in their empire.

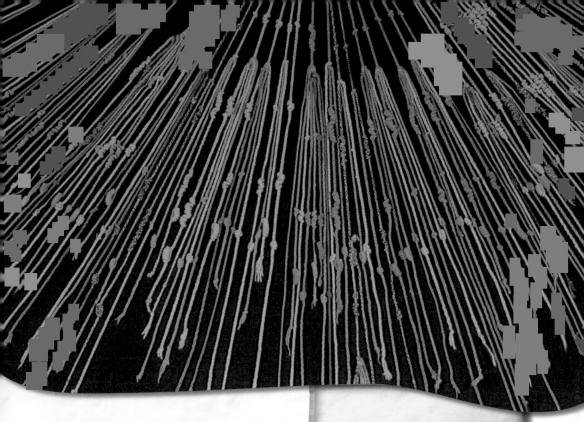

KEEPING A RECORD

Compared with many ancient lands, you'll find the Inca Empire is very well organized. What makes the Inca Empire really impressive is that it is run without writing anything down. The Incas don't have a written langage. Instead, they keep their records on knotted strings called *quipus* (see box).

WHAT ARE QUIPUS?

Quipus are lengths of different coloured knotted string that are attached to one central cord. The colour of the string stands for whatever is being counted (such as warriors or maize), and the various knots stand for different numbers. Special officials, known as *quipu camayocs*, or *quipu* keepers, are taught how to understand the *quipu* system. They use *quipus* to organize everything, including raising armies, building roads, and storing corn.

A UNITED EMPIRE

Being a foreigner in the Inca Empire shouldn't be much of a problem. This is partly because the empire is made up of many different tribes, so the Incas have lots of practice in dealing with foreigners. The Incas also run a clever scheme to mix up all the tribes and make sure that everyone works happily together.

Each time they conquer a new tribe, the Incas send a group of people from the heart of their empire to help the conquered tribe learn their ways. This system works well but it relies on total obedience to the Sapa Inca. Incas have to be prepared at any time to follow orders and move to the newly conquered lands.

LOCAL DIFFERENCES

Although the Incas expect obedience from conquered tribes, they are fairly relaxed in other ways. If you visit the remote parts of the empire you'll notice that the locals seem very different from the Incas in Cuzco. They speak their own dialect, follow their own customs, and worship local gods. So long as all the people in the empire obey the Sapa Inca and agree to worship the god of the sun, they are allowed to continue with their traditional ways of life.

HOW TO GREET AN INCA

When two Incas meet, they greet each other by raising their forefinger to shoulder height and pointing up towards the sky.

NEW CRAFTS

The Inca system of mixing people up works both ways. While a group of Incas moves to the newly conquered lands, another group from the conquered tribe makes the opposite journey to Cuzco. Here, the conquered people teach the Incas their special skills, and this results in a wide range of new Inca crafts. You can see the effects of this system if you visit a goldsmith's workshop. You'll find that he has either come from the north of the empire or he has learnt his skills from a northern goldsmith.

JUST COUNTING

Don't be worried if you notice your group being counted. The Incas love counting people. Because their lands are constantly expanding they carry out frequent **censuses**, when everyone in the empire is counted. This allows them to keep the empire running very smoothly.

Inca gold: this stunning Stone of the Sun is the work of goldsmiths from the north of the empire.

CLOTHES AND CUSTOMS

If you want to fit in with the Incas, you'll need to dress like them. Ordinary farming folk wear a simple tunic, sandals, and a patterned cloak woven from llama wool. Nobles dress in a similar style, but their clothes are made from alpaca wool, which is much softer and finer than llama wool.

BATMAN!

A Spanish visitor to the Inca Empire described the Emperor Atahualpa wearing a cloak made from the skins of vampire bats.

All Incas wear a short tunic and a cloak but the nobleman's clothes are far grander and more colourful.

Nobleman

Farmer

To mix with the nobles, you'll need to wear some large, gold earplugs, but this will involve some pain. Inca earplugs are shaped liked flat, round disks. They fit inside the earlobe, but first the skin of the earlobe has to be split and stretched. The Inca ruling classes also take frequent baths and spend a lot of time on their appearance. Men usually wear their hair long at the back and cut in a fringe at the front. Women plait their long hair into fine braids, which are either worn down the back or wound around the head.

HOW TO BEHAVE

Children in the Inca Empire are expected to be completely obedient and never complain, and they are brought up to be very tough. They are washed in icy water and left out in their cradles on cold nights. As soon as they are old enough, children are taught adult skills. Young boys have to look after animals, collect firewood, and scare away pests in the fields. Young girls have to help their mothers with the younger children. They also learn household tasks, such as cooking and weaving.

EDUCATION

If you end up in the countryside there won't be any school for you! This is because the Sapa Inca believes that too much education is bad for the ordinary working people. However, some children do go to school. In Cuzco, boys from noble families study religion, poetry, arithmetic, and history.

WELCOME TO ADULT LIFE

If you're lucky you may get to see an **initiation** ceremony. This takes place when an Inca boy is around 14 years old. It marks the time when he becomes a man and takes on new work in his family. The boy has his legs whipped hard by all the elders of his *ayllu* (family group). The pain is meant to remind him of his duties to his parents and elders!

RELIGION

Wherever you travel in the Inca Empire, you'll find temples and holy places. The Incas worship a range of gods and goddesses, but the most important of these are Viracocha, the creator, and Inti, the Sun god. Other very important gods are Illapa, god of thunder and lightning, and Pacha Mama, goddess of the Earth.

SUN AND MOON

Inti is believed to be the father of the Sapa Inca and the great protector of the Inca people. Like the Sapa Inca, Inti is married to his sister, Mama Quilla, the Moon. The Coya Inca (see page 13) is believed to be the daughter of the Moon. You'll find a temple to Inti at the heart of all cities and towns.

INCA GODS AT A GLANCE
- Viracocha – the creator
- Inti – god of the Sun
- Mama Quilla – the Moon goddess
- Illapa – god of thunder and lightning
- K'uychi – the rainbow god
- Pacha Mama – goddess of the Earth
- Mama Cocha – goddess of the sea

HOLY PLACES

As well as worshipping the gods, the Incas worship holy places, known as *huacas*. These places can be rocks, caves, springs, and even trees, and all of them are believed to have magical powers. Watch out for *huacas* on your travels. Less important ones will have some offerings of maize beer beside them. More important *huacas* will be guarded by priests and priestesses. These holy places should be approached with care – the Incas make **sacrifices** to the huacas, offering llamas and sometimes even children!

PRIESTS AND PRIESTESSES

Some Incas devote their lives to the gods and become priests and priestesses. If a young girl is especially good and obedient she is taken away from her village and trained to be an *aclla*. These holy women live together in a special house. They serve in temples and weave special clothes for the priests and emperor.

WORSHIPPING THE DEAD

You will need a very strong stomach in the Inca Empire. The Incas spend a lot of time paying their respects to the dead. In Cuzco, the bodies of the dead Sapa Incas are preserved with **embalming** fluids and **mummified**. The mummified emperors are dressed in their royal robes, seated on their thrones, and given maize beer to drink. Meanwhile, all over the empire, people visit the tombs of their **ancestors** to offer them gifts and to ask them for advice.

Even ordinary people mummified their dead, by setting the body out in the cold.

The Incas built walls using massive, interlocking stones that weigh many tons.

CHAPTER 2

CUZCO AND MACHU PICCHU

One of the high points of your trip to the Inca Empire will be a visit to the capital city of Cuzco, in southern Peru. At over 3 kilometres (1.9 miles) above sea level, it's the highest capital city in the ancient world. It's also the cultural centre of the Inca world and is packed with fascinating palaces and temples. You will be amazed – and sometimes horrified – by its spectacular sights.

While you're in Peru don't miss out on a visit to Machu Picchu. This small mountain stronghold is about 100 kilometres (62 miles) north of Cuzco. Perched on a **ridge** between two mountain peaks, it has breathtaking views. Plan to visit Cuzco first and then relax in Machu Picchu.

CUZCO

To the Incas, Cuzco is the sacred home of the gods and the place where all four quarters of the empire meet (see page 14). The most important religious ceremonies are held here, in the spectacular central square.

It's easy to find your way around Cuzco. The city is laid out like a grid, with four major gateways for the four main roads leading to the quarters of the empire. At the heart of the city is an enormous ceremonial square. On the high ground to the north, the towering buildings of the Sacsahuaman fortress look out over the city.

THE GOLDEN ENCLOSURE

First on your list of places to visit must be the *Coricancha*, or golden enclosure. The *Coricancha* is the most **sacred** part of Cuzco. It is very hard to miss because around its outer wall is a band of gold! However, in spite of its gleaming walls it is a simple building, with a straw **thatched** roof.

The *Coricancha* is dedicated to a number of gods, but the most important building there is the temple to Inti, the god of the Sun.

PALACES OF THE DEAD

All around the central square are the royal palaces. These magnificent stone buildings contain many grand rooms, with their tall ceilings supported on pillars of wood. Each royal palace is home to a different emperor, who sits in his throne room. But be prepared for a very nasty shock – almost all of these emperors are dead!

If you are feeling brave, visit the throne room of one of the royal palaces. There you will see the mummified body of a dead emperor seated on a golden stool. At the emperor's side will be his serving women, who serve him food and whisk the flies away from his face!

THE SACSAHUAMAN COMPLEX

The enormous complex of Sacsahuaman is intended to be a **fortress**, and it is defended by three layers of zig-zag walls. It also contains many temples to the gods.

Once you've explored inside the complex, take a close look at its walls. They are constructed from thousands of massive interlocking stones weighing many tons. It has been estimated that over 30,000 men worked for nearly 30 years to build the fortress!

Jigsaw in stone: the city is constructed from many-sided hand-carved blocks like these.

A view of the upper terraces at Machu Picchu, looking towards a circular watchtower.

MACHU PICCHU

You'll never forget your first sight of Machu Picchu, perched on a ridge between two mountain peaks. The city is home to about a thousand people, all living closely packed together. With its temples, palaces, storehouses, and ordinary homes, it's a great place to experience Inca life.

EXPLORING MACHU PICCHU

Machu Picchu is built on steeply rising ground, with its grandest buildings at the top. On the highest ground is the great square, flanked by temples and with spectacular views of the valleys beyond. If you're lucky, you may manage to see a religious ceremony or even watch a military parade in the square.

The most important site in Machu Picchu is the Stone of the Sun. This L-shaped stone stands on a platform at the city's highest point. Also not to be missed while you are in the **plaza** are the circular *torreón* (or watchtowers) and the spectacular Temple of the Three Windows.

Further down the hill you'll find the nobles' palaces with their thick stone walls, and below these, the homes of the city's farmers, labourers, and craft workers. Wander down the narrow streets and peer inside the doorways of these simple one-room homes, with their stone walls and grass-thatched roofs.

While you're in the lower part of town, have a peep inside the large public storehouses, where food and other supplies are stored. You might also be tempted to take a quick tour of the city's dungeons.

OUTSIDE THE TOWN

Outside the city walls there's more to explore. The hillsides are covered with terraced fields. Here you'll see farmers hard at work, growing potatoes and grain. At the base of the fields are the soldiers' **barracks**, while on the eastern side of the hill are burial caves, where citizens go to visit their dead **ancestors**.

The Stone of the Sun is also known as *Intihuatana*, which means "post where the Sun is tied". It casts a strong shadow on the ground and is used by the Inca priests to keep track of the Sun's yearly movements.

Modern Andean people still use colourful dyes for their clothing.

CHAPTER 3

TRAVEL, FOOD, AND SHELTER

For most of your journeys in the Inca Empire, you'll have to rely on your own two feet – the Incas don't have any wheeled vehicles. However, you should be able to find a llama to carry your luggage. Farmers keep herds of llamas in mountain pastures and they are used by nobles, merchants, and farmers for carrying heavy loads. The other good news is that the roads are excellent and there are places to stay along the way.

On lakes and rivers you can travel in canoes made from reeds. This may sound worrying, but don't be scared – reed canoes float very well. And while you're on your travels, you won't go hungry. You'll be able to stock up on plenty of filling food at the rest houses along the roadside.

ON THE MOVE

The Inca Empire has one of the best road systems in the ancient world. There are 25,000 km (15,500 miles) of roads, and many are paved with stone. There are two main highways running parallel to each other, one through the highlands and the other along the coast. They are always full of travellers and their llamas.

BRIDGE THAT GORGE!

Inca roads have to climb steep hills and cross deep river **gorges**. On the hillsides, roads are built in steps. River gorges are crossed by rope bridges made from plaited reeds and anchored at each end to a stone platform. Bridges are sometimes 60 metres (196 feet) long and are just wide enough for two llamas to pass each other. Inca bridges look very scary but there's no need to worry — they are checked regularly by an inspector.

FELLOW TRAVELLERS

While you're on your travels you'll see farmers on their way to market with their llamas laden with produce. Look out for government officials, hurrying from district to district with their bags full of *quipus*.

SPECIAL DELIVERY

Watch out for messengers, known as *chasquis*, on the roads. They run very fast and don't stop for anyone! *Chasquis* run in teams, with new runners waiting at intervals along the road. They wear a headdress of white feathers, and blow on a **conch shell** to warn the next runner to get ready. *Chasquis* carry messages at a speed of up to 320 kilometres (200 miles) a day. They either memorize their messages or carry *quipus*.

If you're really lucky, you might pass the emperor on one of his tours of the empire. The Sapa Inca and his Coya Inca travel in style – sitting in a wooden litter with a feathered roof, which is carried on the shoulders of servants. A grand procession of priests, servants, soldiers, musicians, and dancers accompany the emperor wherever he goes.

PLACES TO STAY

You'll find a range of places to stay in the empire. You may be an honoured guest in an emperor's palace, or join a farming family in their simple home. There are rest houses along the main highways, known as *tambos*. These are simple stone houses with thatched roofs, specially designed for travellers to spend the night and stock up on food and drink.

This 19th century painting shows the remains of a luxurious Inca palace.

PALACES

Inca palaces can be very grand, especially if they belong to an emperor. You might see a grand entrance and massive reception halls. One advantage of Inca palaces is their plumbing. You will be able to enjoy a dip in a stone bath filled with water piped from a hot spring.

SIMPLE HOMES

Most houses in the Inca Empire are simple buildings with a thatched grass roof. Their walls are made from stone or adobe, mud bricks mixed with grass. Inca homes have one entrance covered with a cloth and (sometimes) a small, high window. Clay stoves provide heat in cold weather. There are no chimneys – smoke just rises up through the thatch, so be prepared for a draughty, smoky experience!

Inside the house you may find a stone bench, some **niches** in the wall, and stone pegs for hanging up clothes. You will be expected to sleep on the floor on reed mats or llama skins. You'll find some cold spring water running in a stone channel outside the house for washing.

SHOCKPROOF BUILDINGS

Most large Inca buildings are made from interlocking granite blocks, with no cement to stick them together. The blocks fit together so well that even when they are shaken by an earthquake they usually fall back into position. The Incas use small hand-held hammer stones to shape their blocks. (If you look carefully at an Inca granite wall, you will see the marks made by the hammer stones.)

NO PRIVACY

Don't expect any privacy in an Inca home – everyone sleeps and eats together in the same room. Houses are usually grouped around a central courtyard. Here the women do their cooking and weaving whilst people hang out and chat with members of their family.

Don't be surprised if an official drops by to check up on you. Inca houses are inspected by officials twice a year.

You will probably stay in a simple Inca home like this. Don't expect many comforts – just concentrate on the amazing view!

WHAT TO EAT

Inca food varies depending on where you are in the empire. In the highlands, the Incas grow more than 200 different varieties of potatoes. Potatoes are usually made into a thick soup. On the plains, maize is grown in very large quantities. Maize is sometimes eaten as corn on the cob or baked, to make a form of popcorn. It's also ground into flour to make bread, porridge, and dumplings.

All the Incas, from the emperor downwards, like to drink maize beer, or *chicha*. It tastes pretty strange but the worst thing about chicha is the way it's made. First, old women chew the grains of maize very thoroughly. Then they spit the mush into jars of warm water, where it **ferments** and turns into beer! *Chicha* is usually stored in large ceramic pots sunk into the ground, and is drunk from colourful drinking cups called *qeros*.

Incas love hot and spicy food such as chillies and garlic.

ADDING VARIETY

Apart from potatoes and maize, the Incas grow beans and vegetables, which they make into stews, with added chillis for flavour. In the mountains, farmers grow root vegetables. In the lower, flatter parts of the empire, the main crops are squashes and tomatoes. Most Inca families eat very little meat, although they sometimes add birds, frogs, and even worms to their stews! People on the coast eat a lot of fish.

If you want a really varied diet, you'll have to join the emperor and his nobles. Their food is **imported** from all over the empire. When you dine in a royal palace you can expect to enjoy a wide range of cooked fish and birds, as well as tropical fruit such as bananas. Even though Cuzco is nearly 480 kilometres (300 miles) from the Pacific Ocean, you can still enjoy fresh fish in an Inca noble's home. The nobles use the excellent road system to get their fish delivered within 24 hours.

LOVE YOUR LLAMA!

Many farmers keep llamas, but they rarely use them for their meat. That's because llamas are much too useful to be eaten. Farmers use llamas to carry heavy loads and to supply wool for weaving. Even the llamas' dung is used. It can be spread on the ground as **fertilizer**, or dried and used as fuel for fires.

TASTY TREATS!

Many Inca families have guinea pigs running round their houses, but they don't think of them as pets. The guinea pigs are allowed to feed off plants and kitchen scraps until they're nice and fat, and then the family eats them as a treat!

Andean people still wear traditional ceremonial dress to celebrate Inca festivals in Cuzco today.

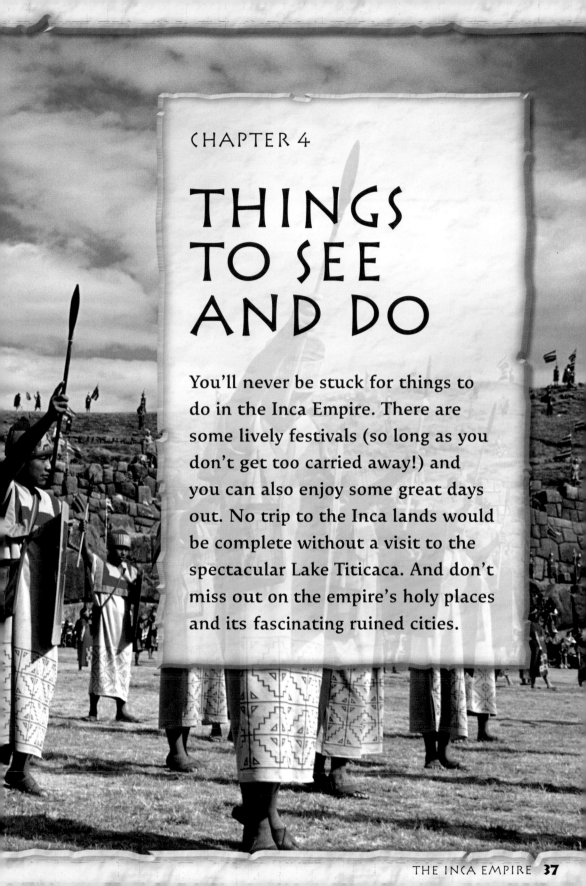

CHAPTER 4

THINGS TO SEE AND DO

You'll never be stuck for things to do in the Inca Empire. There are some lively festivals (so long as you don't get too carried away!) and you can also enjoy some great days out. No trip to the Inca lands would be complete without a visit to the spectacular Lake Titicaca. And don't miss out on the empire's holy places and its fascinating ruined cities.

FESTIVALS AND FUN

The Incas work very hard but they also like to have fun. Families celebrate births and marriages and there are many religious festivals throughout the year. While you're in the Inca Empire, make sure you join in some of these events. You'll see some sights you'll never forget!

MAKING MUSIC

The Incas don't have any stringed instruments but they do have whistles, drums, bells, and rattles. They also blow loudly on conch shells, and play tunes on panpipes made from bamboo canes tied together.

THE FESTIVAL OF THE SUN

Inti Raymi, the festival of the Sun, is the biggest celebration of the year. It is held in Cuzco at the end of the maize harvest. Before the Sun rises on the day of the festival, all the mummified emperors are carried into the plaza and seated on golden thrones. The plaza is filled with the dead emperors' servants and all the Inca nobles, dressed in silver and gold.

Look out for people playing conch shell trumpets!

The Sapa Inca leads a chant to welcome the Sun as it rises. This is the start of a day of celebration, which includes music, dancing, feasting, and military parades. At the end of the day all the Incas bow low in sadness to the departing Sun.

CHASING AFTER THE RIVER

Mayucati, which means "chasing after the river", takes place in January. **Ashes** from animal sacrifices are thrown into the swollen river in Cuzco, at the height of the rainy season. Teenage boys chase the ashes down the river half way to Machu Picchu. They then race each other back to Cuzco.

TEENAGE TESTS

The feast of *Capac Raymi* held in mid-December is a fast-moving spectacle, and an endurance test for teenage boys. It's very exciting to watch, but don't be tempted to join in. You could easily end up dead!

The test begins with a group of teenage boys spending several nights on a freezing mountain top, learning the legends of their ancestors. Then they descend to Cuzco to perform a special dance. After this, they race each other up and down four different mountain peaks. On the twenty-first day, the boys who have survived are dressed in fine clothes and have their earlobes split, ready to be given their golden earplugs – the sign that they have become an adult.

Women offering plates of food at *Inti Raymi*, the festival of the Sun which is held in Cuzco once a year.

GREAT DAYS OUT

There are many fascinating places to visit in the Inca Empire. First on your list, after Cuzco and Machu Picchu, should be a trip to Lake Titicaca. You could also plan a trip to the sacred spring at Tambo Machay. Or, to get a feel for a completely different part of the empire, why not travel to Pachacamac on the coast?

LAKE TITICACA

Lake Titicaca is a truly stunning sight, with its deep turquoise waters framed by the snow-capped peaks of the Andes Mountains. At 3,800 metres (12,468 feet) above sea level, it is the highest lake in the world and is used for fishing and boating. Lake Titicaca is also a holy place for the Incas (see box).

THE LEGEND OF VIRACOCHA

The Incas believe that their god Viracocha lived in the waters of Lake Titicaca when the world was dark. At the time of the creation, Viracocha emerged from the lake and created the Sun and the Moon. After this, he created the first human beings, but they annoyed the god so they were changed to stone. Then Viracocha made a second group of humans and travelled across the world calling them into being. Viracocha travelled until he reached the Pacific coast, but then he disappeared over the ocean.

Take a canoe ride across Lake Titicaca to view the sacred islands of the Sun and Moon. ❯

Every year, hundreds of Incas make the **pilgrimage** to see Lake Titicaca and to visit the sacred islands of the Sun and Moon. You may even be able to join in a voyage to the islands. Here, Inca officials will guide you around the islands' temples and **observatories**, and you will be able to see **astronomer**-priests at work, studying the movements of the Sun, Moon, and stars.

TAMBO MACHAY

Close to Cuzco is the sacred spring of Tambo Machay. This is an example of a *huaca*, or sacred place (see page 20). Here, the Incas have built an impressive open-air shrine with carved stone basins to catch the holy water. If you decide to visit this *huaca*, take a gift of maize beer to offer to the god.

PACHACAMAC

Pachacamac on the central coast of Peru is a place of pilgrimage for the Incas. They believe that this is the home of the god of the Earth, who lives off the coast, deep in the ocean. There are many magnificent temples overlooking the sea.

Pilgrims travel to Pachacamac to receive messages from their god. If you join the crowds of pilgrims, you can ask the god your own question. All your questions have to be asked through the *acllas* (female priests) who guard the temple.

ON THE HISTORY TRAIL

While you're in ancient South America, take time to visit the remains of some of the earlier great civilizations. These earlier people had a powerful influence on the Inca way of life.

PEOPLE OF THE ANDES

Around 1000 BC, the Chavin people developed a thriving civilization in the Andes mountains. They built huge stone temples and discovered how to make things from gold. The Chavin were followed by a series of great civilizations, including the Paracas, the Moche, and the Chimu. By the time you visit the Inca Empire, all these early civilizations will be in ruins. But you will still be able to visit their crumbling cities and see how they influenced the Inca people.

CIVILIZATIONS OF THE ANDES

(Note: dates given are approximate.)

1000–300 BC	The Chavin rule northern and central Peru
1000 BC–AD 400	The Paracas rule southern Peru
AD 1–700	The Moche rule northern Peru
AD 400–600	The Nazca rule southern Peru
AD 600–1200	The Tiahuanacos rule Bolivia and southern Peru
AD 550–1000	The Wari – a rival empire to Tiahuanaco throughout Peru
AD 1200–1471	The Chimu rule northern Peru
AD 1300–1532	The Incas rule all the Andes region

CHAN CHAN

The city of Chan Chan was the capital of the Chimu Empire in northern Peru. The Chimu people were defeated by the Incas in the 1470s.

Hammered gold was a feature of Chimu craft. ↘

The city of Chan Chan has similarities with the Inca capital at Cuzco. Chan Chan is an impressive city, made up of many separate fortresses surrounded by high walls. At the heart of each fortress is a ceremonial square with the remains of grand temples and palaces. On the outskirts of Chan Chan there are many smaller houses for craft workers and farmers.

TIAHUANACO

The ruined ancient city of Tiahuanaco, close to Lake Titicaca, is a place of wonder for the Incas. This city was built around 200 BC, and taken over by a series of later peoples. By the time the Incas conquered Tiahuanaco around 1470, the great city was already in ruins, but the Incas were amazed by its massive buildings and its fine stonework. Emperor Pachacuti took note of the construction methods used in Tiahuanaco so that he could copy them in his capital city. He even brought stonemasons from Tiahuanaco to help construct some of the fabulous buildings in Cuzco.

Paracas weavers combined great colours with elaborate designs. These skills were kept alive in the Inca Empire.

CRAFT TRADITIONS

The Inca crafts of weaving, pottery, and metalwork have been strongly influenced by the traditions of earlier civilizations. The Paracas people of southern Peru developed the skill of dyeing and weaving llama wool to create colourful patterned cloth. The northern Moche people specialized in making pottery drinking pots in the form of warriors, and the Chimu people created ornaments and masks from hammered gold. All these skills and traditions can be seen in the craft works of the Incas.

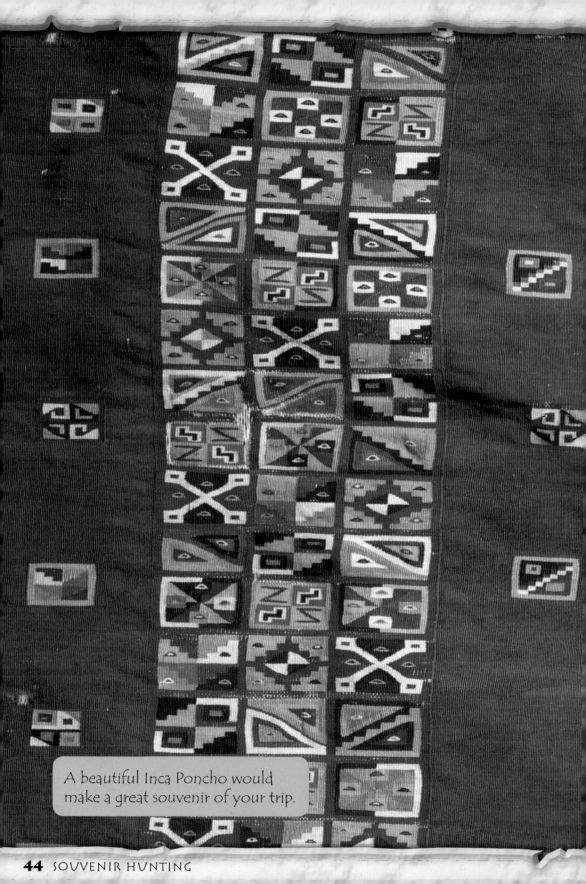

A beautiful Inca Poncho would make a great souvenir of your trip.

CHAPTER 5

SOUVENIR HUNTING

You can find some brilliant souvenirs of your trip, but don't expect to find them in a shop or market. The Incas don't use money and they don't encourage people to exchange goods. Inca craft workers make just enough items to meet their people's needs. They also produce luxury goods for the emperor and his nobles as part of their duty of service to the empire. So, if you wish to leave the Inca lands with some fine examples of crafts in your luggage, you'll have to make friends with some weavers and silversmiths!

WHAT TO TAKE HOME

The Incas are famous for their weaving and metalwork, so these should be your first choice of souvenirs. But other good choices would be a musical instrument (see page 38) or a colourful drinking cup called a *qeros* (see page 34). The Incas make their cups from pottery or wood and decorate them with bold designs. Some cups are even shaped like animals.

INCA WEAVING

Top of your list of souvenirs must be an example of Inca weaving. But the problem is, what do you choose? Inca weavers make a wide range of goods, including blankets, cloaks, tunics, headdresses, and belts. Most of these garments are dyed brilliant colours (see box) and decorated with striking patterns.

Inca textiles are famous for their stunning colours and patterns. This is part of a noble's tunic.

BRILLIANT COLOURS

Inca weavers use dyes made from plants, shells, and insects to colour their wool. Two favourite colours are a bright scarlet made from the bodies of the crushed cochineal beetle, and a deep blue made from the indigo plant.

Inca weaving comes in three different textures. The thickest and coarsest cloth is woven from llamas' fleece. This is what the ordinary people use for their clothes. The finer, softer cloth is made from alpaca fleece, and this is the usual choice for nobles. The softest and lightest wool comes from the fleece of the vicuna, a smaller relative of the llama. This cloth is woven by the *aclla* (female priests) for the Sapa Inca and his family.

Some of the finest patterns can be seen on the Inca tunics. These are usually scattered with small **geometric** designs. Weaving these delicate patterns into the cloth requires great skill, and the smaller the pattern, the greater the weaver's skill. If a tunic has a band of pattern across the waist, it has been made for someone of noble birth. The band is called a *tocapu*, and it sometimes shows the special design of the wearer's family.

INCA METALWORK

Inca goldsmiths and silversmiths make striking jewellery for the emperor, priests, and nobles. These stunning objects usually take the form of earplugs, breastplates, and military medals. Sometimes, hundreds of small gold or silver plates are sown onto tunics and cloaks to make them glitter in the sun. Goldsmiths also hammer gold into masks, for priests to wear at festivals.

While you are visiting the Inca temples, you may see some model llamas, made from solid silver or gold. These precious objects are gifts for the gods, so don't try to take one home with you!

How about giving your dad a cup with a snarling jaguar's head?

You will see amazing views of high mountains and deep lakes, but be careful if you go exploring!

CHAPTER 6

HEALTH AND SAFETY

The Inca Empire is strictly not for wimps! Visitors to the empire need strong legs, a good head for heights, and a sound pair of lungs. But you don't need to worry too much about falling ill. The Incas have some excellent doctors, and if you are sick or elderly you can expect kind treatment. The Inca Empire is also very well run, so most of the time you should feel pretty safe.

HEALTH ADVICE

Travellers to the Inca Empire should be prepared for some exhausting and dangerous climbs. You will also have to get used to the thin mountain air. Most foreign visitors to Machu Picchu suffer from **altitude** sickness – a feeling of weakness, breathlessness, and nausea.

Many travellers also find it hard to adjust to the dramatic changes in temperature – from hot and steamy rainforests to freezing mountain-tops.

VISITING A DOCTOR

If you do fall ill, you will need to visit a doctor – called a *hampi camayoc*. Inca doctors are experts at curing fevers and dressing wounds. To help them in their task, they use a range of medicines and ointments made from rainforest plants.

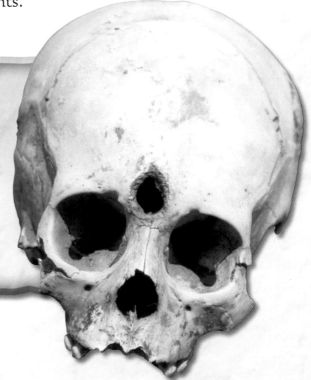

HOLE IN THE HEAD

You'd better not complain of a headache while you're in the Inca Empire. Some Inca doctors practise a technique called trepanning. This involves making a hole in a patient's skull to drain off fluid from the brain.

If you need an operation, there are also plenty of skilled surgeons in the Inca Empire. And don't worry too much about the pain. The Incas have some powerful pain-killing drugs, such as quinine, coca leaves, or strong cactus beer.

Inca doctors are excellent at curing **dysentery** and tropical diseases. But don't expect them to be able to treat you for flu. When the Incas caught influenza from the Spanish soldiers their doctors were powerless to cure them.

MAINLY MAGIC

If the Inca doctors can't cure you, you could try visiting a shaman instead. Shamans are healers who rely on magic, and they usually live in remote mountain caves. Once you've reached the shaman you can expect to take part in a mysterious **ritual** to drive out evil spirits from your body. Rituals usually involve **trances**, chants, and spells. You will probably also need to take along a llama or a guinea pig, to be sacrificed to the gods.

A visit to an Inca shaman can be a scary experience!

> Even a small town like Machu Picchu has prison buildings and dungeons to keep its lawbreakers out of trouble.

STAYING SAFE

The Incas are a very law-abiding people, so most of the time you should feel pretty safe. However, there are times when you should act with care – so follow the simple guidelines below.

TRIAL AND PUNISHMENT

If you break the law while you're in the Inca Empire, you will be tried by a local government official. He will hear the evidence against you, decide if you are guilty, and carry out your punishment.

Convicted criminals may be stoned or clubbed to death, or tied to a wooden frame and left out in the desert to be eaten by vultures. Sometimes, criminals are hung by their hair over a cliff, until they finally fall to their death.

KEEPING WATCH

Government inspectors keep a very close watch on the Inca people to make sure they work hard and obey the law. This means you should not be at risk from any Incas – they will be much too busy to bother with you. However, you might have to watch out for the inspectors. They might decide that sightseeing is not a valuable use of your time!

DREADFUL DUNGEONS

Whatever you do, don't insult the Sapa Inca. People who commit this crime are sent to an underground chamber filled with snakes, pumas, jaguars, and other wild creatures. Then they are left for three days at the mercy of the animals. If anyone survives this trial, the person is let out and pardoned.

BATTLE ALERT

The Incas are fierce fighters and use some deadly weapons, so make sure you stay well away from battlefields. Battles usually take place on the empire's borders, as the Incas fight against other tribes to win more land. Inca warriors fight with spears, battleaxes, and heavy maces (a kind of club). Some members of the army fight with bows and arrows, while others use slings to fire rocks at their enemies.

CHILDREN BEWARE!

Usually the Incas choose llamas or guinea pigs to sacrifice to their gods, but in times of emergency the Inca people decide that the Sapa Inca needs extra strength. Then some children are taken to the top of a mountain and put to death. Priests usually choose children aged about 10 years, so watch out for Incas who want to take you up high mountains!

This Inca has chosen a llama to sacrifice this time, but watch out they don't choose you!

Llamas are probably the most important animals in Inca culture.

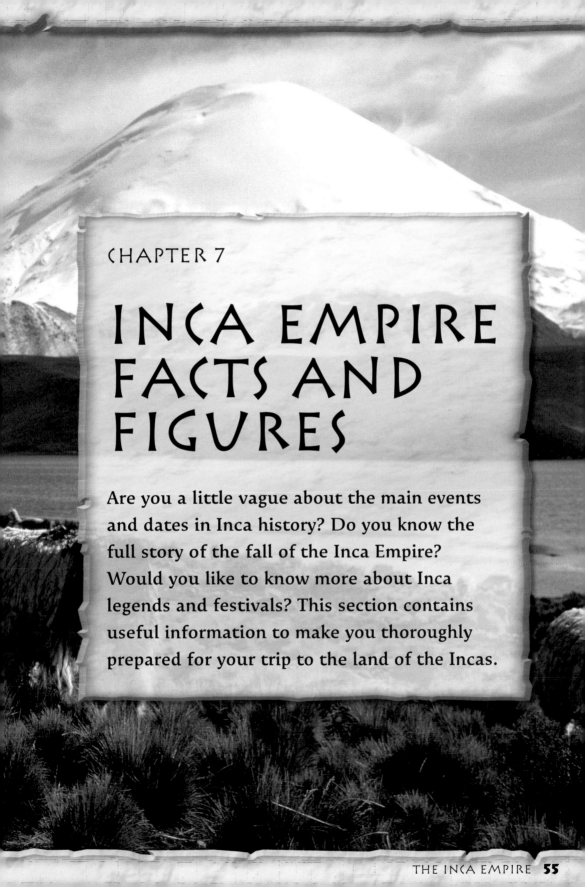

CHAPTER 7

INCA EMPIRE FACTS AND FIGURES

Are you a little vague about the main events and dates in Inca history? Do you know the full story of the fall of the Inca Empire? Would you like to know more about Inca legends and festivals? This section contains useful information to make you thoroughly prepared for your trip to the land of the Incas.

COMMON INCA WORDS

The Inca people speak Quechua, a language that is still spoken in South America today. When you're pronouncing Inca words, remember to follow the guidelines below.

PRONUNCIATION GUIDE

- **HUA** sounds like **WA**
- **QUI** sounds like **KEE**
- The letter **I** is pronounced **EE**
- The letter **Q** is pronounced like **K**, in the back of the throat
- The letter **V** is pronounced **W**

(Stress the **syllable** in _underline_.)

English	Quechua	Pronouced
doctor	hampi camayoc	_hahm_-pee qah-_ma_-yoc
emperor	Sapa	_Sa_-pah
emperor's chief wife	Coya	_Qoi_-ah
family group	ayllu	_eye_-lyoo
festival	raymi	_rye_-_mee_
holy place	huaca	_wah_-kah
knotted record	quipu	_khee_-pooh
messenger	chasqui	_chah_-skee

Names and places

Huayna Capac	_Why_-nah _Qah_-pahk
Topa Inca	Too-pa _Ing_-kah
Tupac Amaru	Too-pahk Ah-_mah_-roo
Cuzco	_Qos_-qoh
Machu Picchu	_Mah_-choo Pee-choo
Pachacamac	Pah-cha-_kah_-mahk
Sacsahuaman	Sax-ah-_wah_-_man_
Tiahuanaco	Tee-ah-wan-_ah_-koo
Coricancha	Qoh-ree-_kahn_-cha

SOME IMPORTANT INCA RULERS

- Pachacuti Inca (1438–1471): began to build up the empire; conquered lands in the north.
- Topa Inca (1471–1493): continued to build up the empire in the north and south.
- Huayna Capac (1493–1525): gained more lands for the empire in the north.
- Atahualpa Inca (1525–1533): captured and killed by Francisco Pizarro (see page 58).
- Manco Capac II (1533–1545): ruled as a **puppet emperor** for the Spaniards, then escaped and set up a rival empire; led an unsuccessful rebellion.
- Tupac Amaru (1571–1572): the last Sapa Inca; murdered by Spanish soldiers.

GUIDE TO FESTIVALS

Some of the major Inca festivals are listed here. Turn to pages 38–39 for more on festivals. (Note that the Inca Empire is in the southern hemisphere, so December is midsummer and June is midwinter).

January *Mayucati* (chasing after the river)
June 21st (winter solstice) *Inti Raymi* (the festival of the Sun)
September *Coya Raymi* (cleansing the city)
November *Aya Marqa* (Festival of the Dead)
December 21st (summer solstice) *Capac Raymi* (teenage initiation ceremony)

THE END OF THE INCAS

In 1532 the Spanish adventurer Francisco Pizarro landed on the north coast of Peru with less than 260 soldiers. He immediately set off inland searching for gold and treasures. Pizarro defeated the Incas in a fierce battle in northern Peru and took Emperor Atahualpa prisoner.

PIZARRO'S TRICK

Pizarro agreed to release Atahualpa if the Incas would pay a ransom in silver and gold. The Incas stripped Cuzco of its treasures, and presented them to Pizarro who started to melt them down. But, instead of releasing Atahualpa as they had promised, the Spaniards kept the emperor imprisoned and eventually put him to death. Then they marched towards the city of Cuzco, defeating several Inca armies on their way.

SPANISH CONQUERORS

The Spanish conquistadors easily took control of Cuzco. In order to gain the support of the Incas, Pizarro set up Manco Capac II (Atahualpa's half-brother) as emperor, but the Spaniards were really in charge. For the next four years the Spaniards controlled the empire, but allowed the Incas to continue to hold their ceremonies.

FRANCISCO PIZARRO (AROUND 1475–1541)

Francisco Pizarro was the son of a Spanish gentleman. In 1510 he joined a ship heading for Colombia, South America. Pizarro learnt about the wealth of the Inca Empire and, in 1524, led an expedition there. His third and final expedition into Inca territory, in 1532, led to the fall of the empire. Once he had gained control of Cuzco, Pizarro set up a new capital city in Lima. He divided the Inca lands amongst his fellow Spaniards but this led to bitter quarrels. In 1541, Pizarro was killed by the followers of one of his Spanish rivals.

In 1536, Manco Capac II managed to escape from Cuzco and was eventually to lead a rebellion against the Spaniards. After several months of attacking the Spaniards, the Inca rebels abandoned Cuzco and retreated to the rainforest. There, a small band of Incas set up a rival kingdom. This continued until 1572, when one of Manco's descendants, Tupac Amaru, was finally captured and executed in public in Cuzco's main square.

THE END OF THE INCA EMPIRE

The death of Tupac Amaru, the last Sapa Inca, marked the end of the Inca Empire. But in fact the empire was already in ruins. Spanish troops had taken over all the towns, set up a new capital in Lima, and divided the Incas' lands between them. They also forced the Inca people to work for them in their fields and mines. During the 16th century, many thousands of Incas died from harsh treatment by Spanish settlers. Thousands more were wiped out by smallpox, measles, and influenza – diseases brought to South America by the Spaniards.

INCAS TODAY

The Inca lands were ruled by Spain until the 19th century, when the countries of South America finally gained their independence. Today, there are many descendants of the Incas still living in Peru, Ecuador, Bolivia, and Chile.

INCA HISTORY AT A GLANCE

(Note: dates given are approximate.)

1200	The Incas start to settle in the Cuzco valley
	According to Inca legend, Manco Capac I founds the city of Cuzco
1400s	The Incas gradually create the city-state of Cuzco
1438	Pachacuti Inca starts to build an empire
1471	Pachacuti and his son, Topa Inca, defeat the Chimu (see pages 42–43) and take over their lands in the north
1492	Christopher Columbus reaches the Americas
1493	Topa Inca conquers the southern part of the empire
	Huayna Capac becomes Sapa Inca. During his reign he wins more lands in the north and the empire reaches its greatest size
1525	Huayna Capac dies and civil war breaks out between his two sons and their supporters
1532	Atahualpa becomes Sapa Inca after defeating his brother in civil war
	Spanish troops led by Francisco Pizarro arrive in northern Peru
	The Spaniards capture Atahualpa
1533	The Spaniards kill Atahualpa and march to Cuzco
	Manco Capac II is crowned as Sapa Inca, but is controlled by the Spaniards
1536	Manco Capac II leads an unsuccessful uprising against the Spaniards
1572	Tupac Amaru, the last Inca emperor, is executed by the Spaniards. The Inca lands are ruled by Spain

FURTHER READING

BOOKS

Inca Life, David Drew (Snapping Turtle Guide) (Ticktock Entertainment, 2003)

Step into the Inca World, Philip Steele (Lorenz Books, 2000)

WEBSITES

- http://en.wikipedia.org/wiki/Inca
  Good general information on the Inca Empire
- http://www.jqjacobs.net/andes/tupac_amaru.html
  The life, times, and execution of the last Inca
- http://www.destination360.com/peru/machu-picchu.php
  360 degree films of Inca artifacts and Peruvian landscapes

GLOSSARY

altitude height

ancestor family members who lived a very long time ago

astronomer someone who studies the stars and the planets

barracks buildings where soldiers live

census official count of all the people living in a country

city-state city that has its own rulers and laws

civil war war between different groups of people in the same country

conch shell large sea shell that can be blown to make a loud, deep noise

conquistador soldier who conquers land and people in a foreign land

convict to find someone guilty of a crime

drought long period of very dry weather

dysentery serious stomach disease that causes people to have very bad diarrhoea and a high temperature

embalm to treat a dead body with ointments so that it does not decay

embroider to sew a design or a picture onto cloth

famine serious shortage of food

ferment to change and turn into alcohol

fertile good for growing plants and crops

fertilizer substance put on the land to make it richer so better crops can be grown

fortress building that is made very strong so that it can resist attacks

geometric shaped like a square or a triangle

gorge very deep valley

import to bring foreign goods into a country to be sold

initiation time when young people become adults and they are introduced to adult society

litter seat with poles attached to it so that it can be carried

mine to dig underground in order to find precious metals

mummify to preserve a dead body by treating it with special ointments and wrapping it in cloth

niche hollow place in a wall

observatory building used by astronomers to study the stars

pasture land where animals can feed and wander around

pilgrimage journey to a holy place

plaza grand open square in a town or city

puppet emperor emperor who is controlled by somebody else

ridge narrow, raised piece of land

ritual set of actions that are performed as part of a religious ceremony

root vegetables vegetables, such as potatoes, that are grown underground

sacred holy

sacrifice animal or human that is killed as a gift for the gods

smallpox serious disease, which causes people to have a very high temperature and to be covered in spots

syllable one of the sounds in a word

terrace field cut out of a hillside like a step

thatched made from straw or reeds

trance dream-like state when you do not know exactly what is going on

tropical hot and steamy

INDEX